THEOREM

THEOREM

Elizabeth Bradfield & Antonia Contro

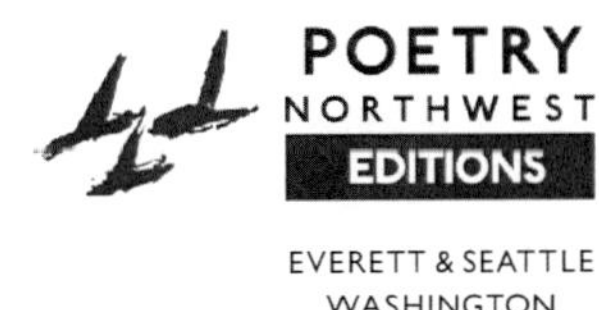

EVERETT & SEATTLE
WASHINGTON

All images by Antonia Contro
Book design by Natalie Mills Bontumasi

Poetry NW Editions is an independent, non-profit educational press in residence
at Everett Community College.

LIBRARY OF CONGRESS CONTROL NUMBER: 2020933321
Names: Bradfield, Elizabeth, and Contro, Antonia, authors
Title: Theorem / Elizabeth Bradfield and Antonia Contro
Description: First Edition / Everett, Washington: Poetry NW Editions, 2020
ISBN-13: 978-1-949166-02-6

Poetry NW Editions
2000 Tower Street
Everett, Washington 98201

www.poetrynw.org

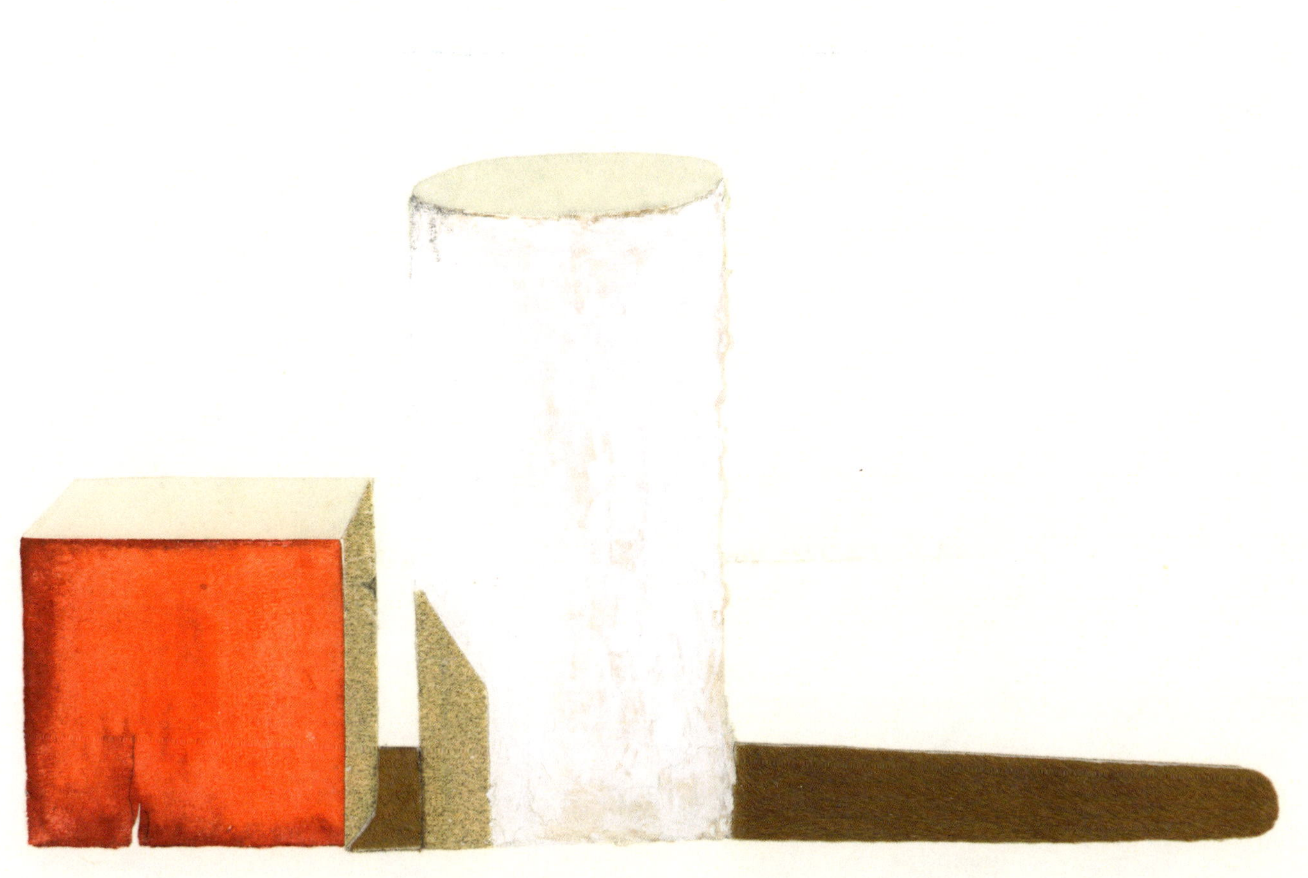

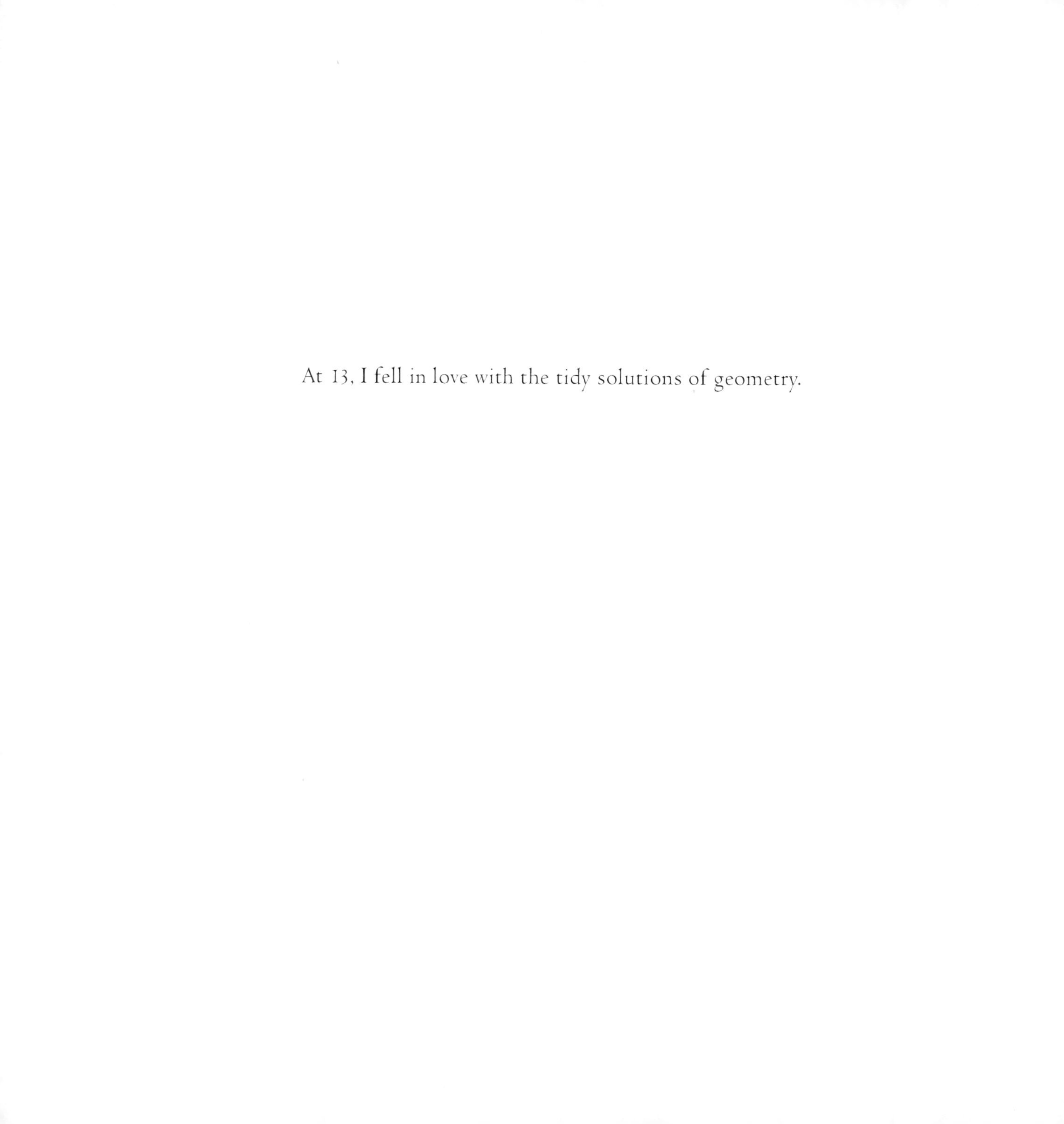

At 13, I fell in love with the tidy solutions of geometry.

Neat in my notebooks, they made architecture of chaos, denoted

all I could not allow myself to say—

                                        contained it in measurable forms.

Yet something pulsed.

Formulas and proofs were fingers caged around a bright, quick thing trapped but not bruised. Not even close. But bruisable. A sort of bird.

This is a story of a secret. Of secrets.

Of becoming from and alongside them.

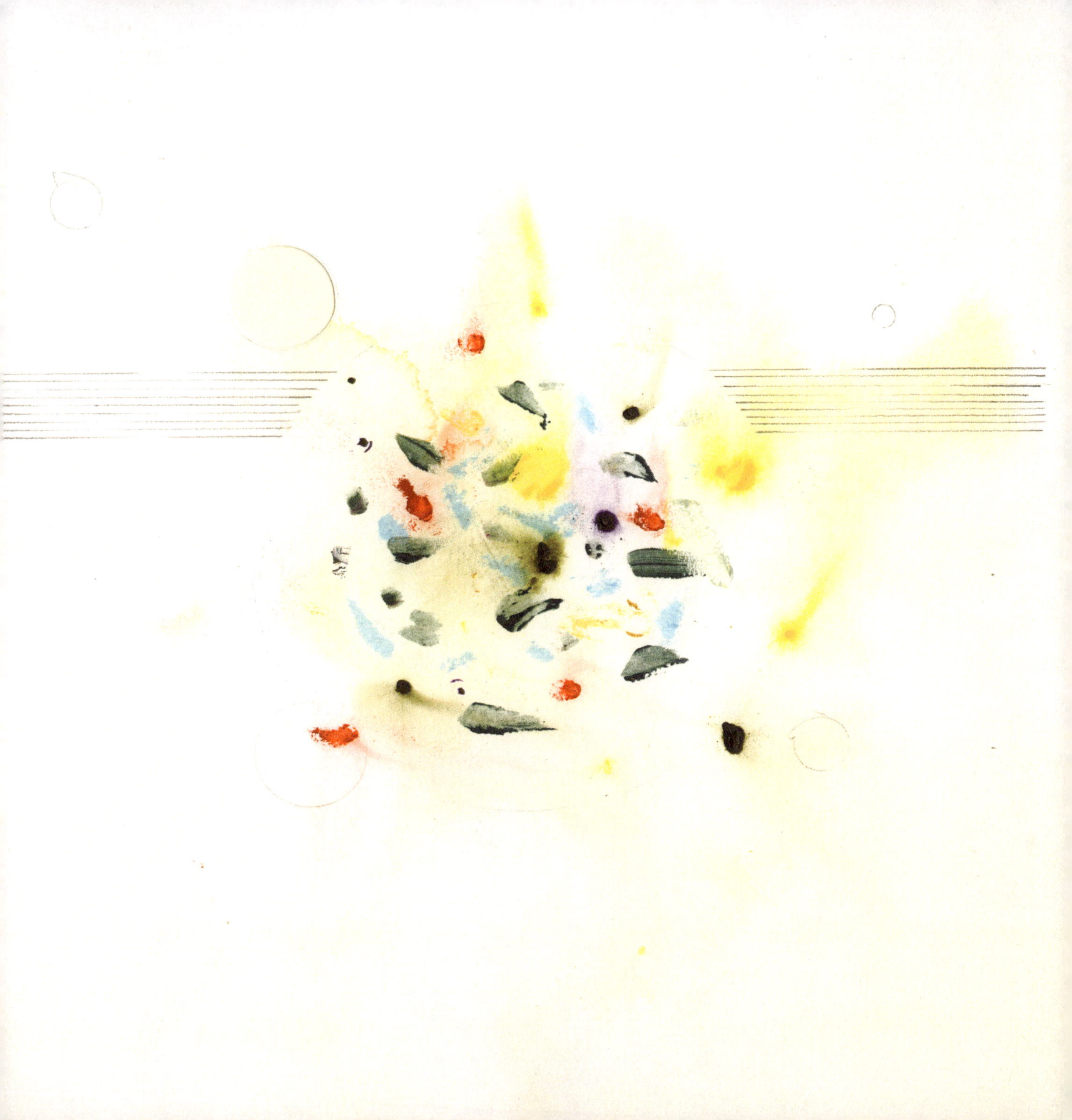

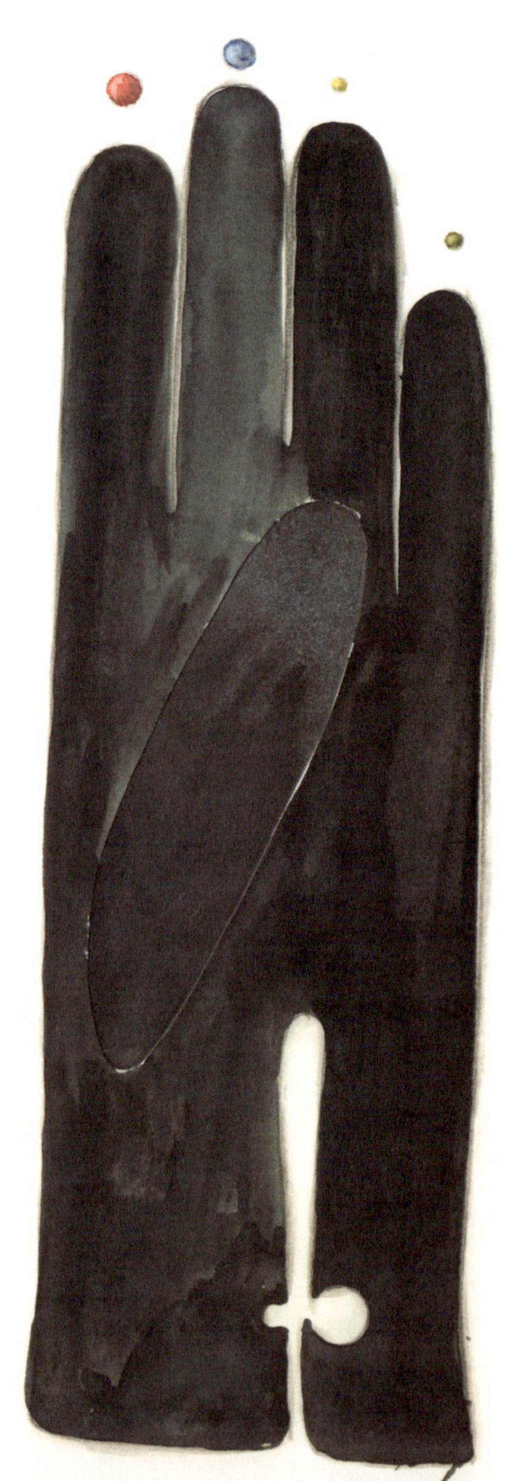

What could allow me to approach myself (my secrets) safely?

Even now (even now) they have power.

As for one,

something had begun to flow through my body's passages.

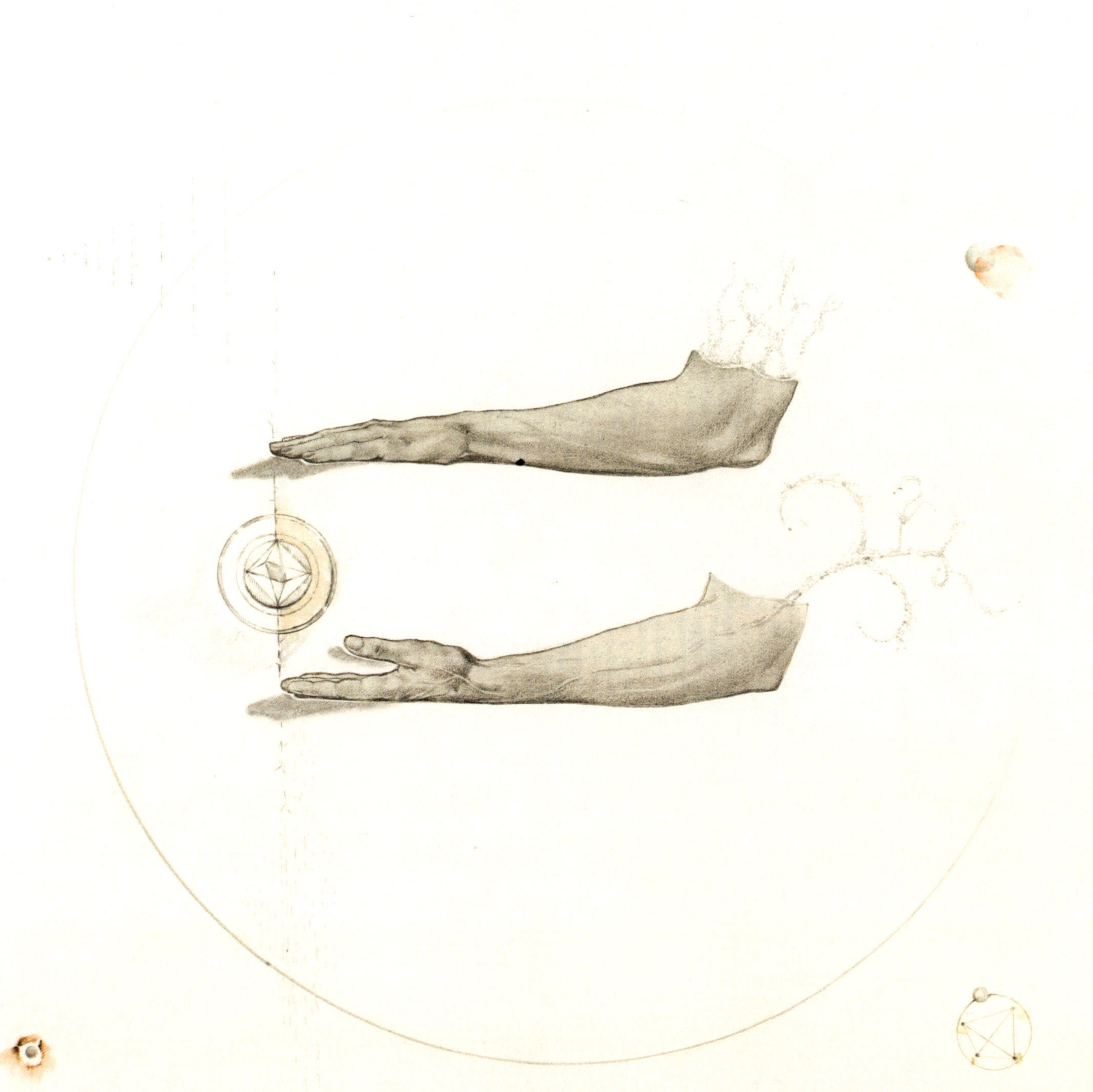

If I opened my hands, what would be revealed?

I knew.

Dark matter.

Strange attractions.

An unknown universe.

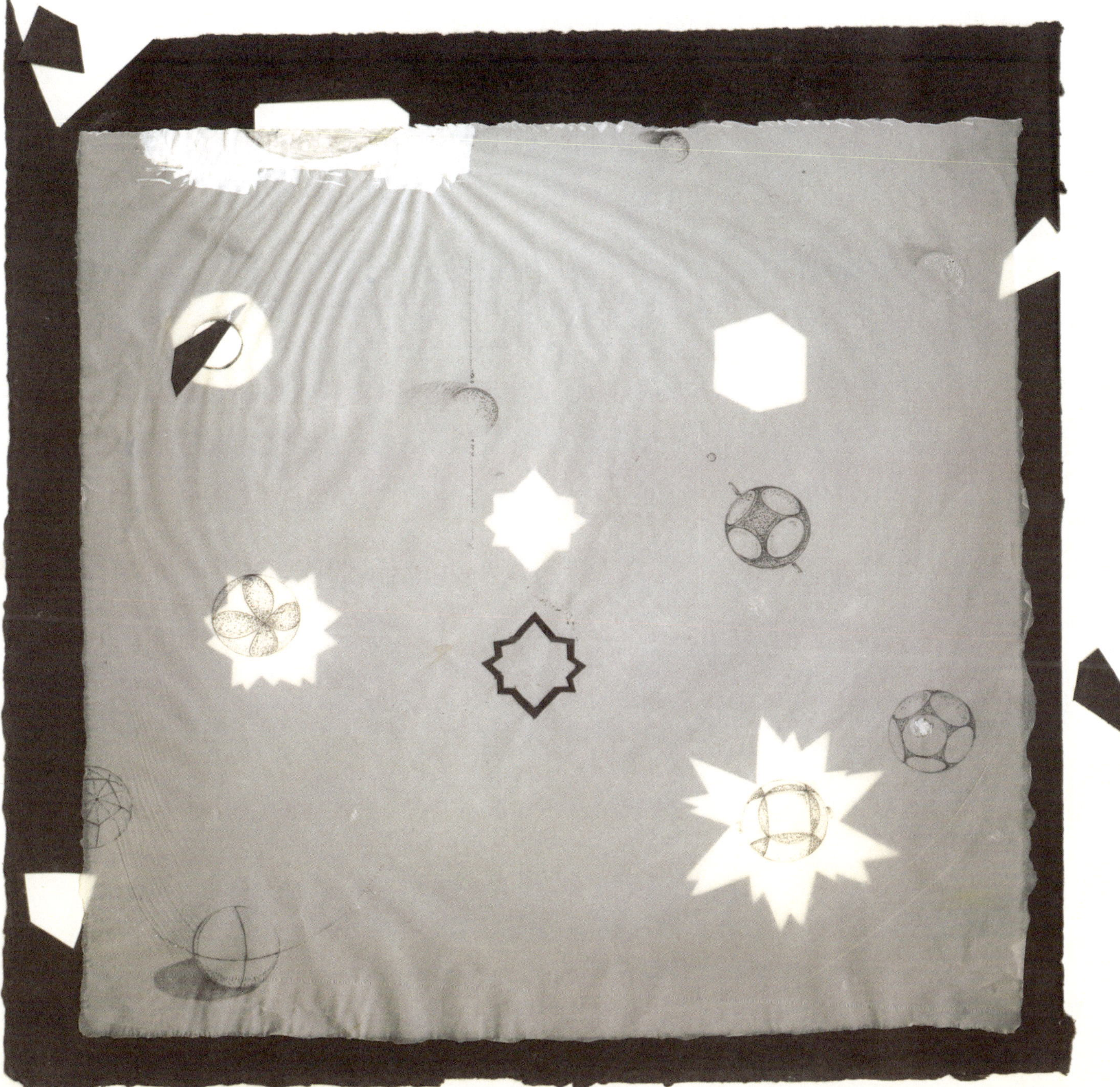

Was it safe?

I didn't know. But stars shone there. I sensed them. And they were not tired,
told fate but a projected escape

                                   —math made map—

        a sky-blanketing that could open and open to the breathless unheld.

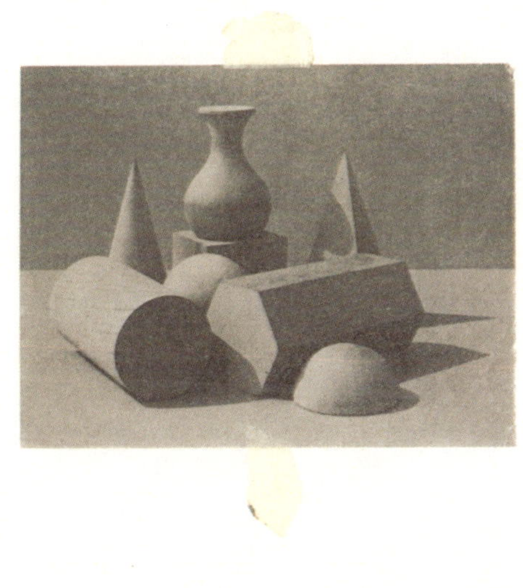

Fig. 3

There were five of us—plus the dog and the dog that died—no others.

I was one of three sisters.

For so long, I didn't know what shape I was.

Did I have to have one?

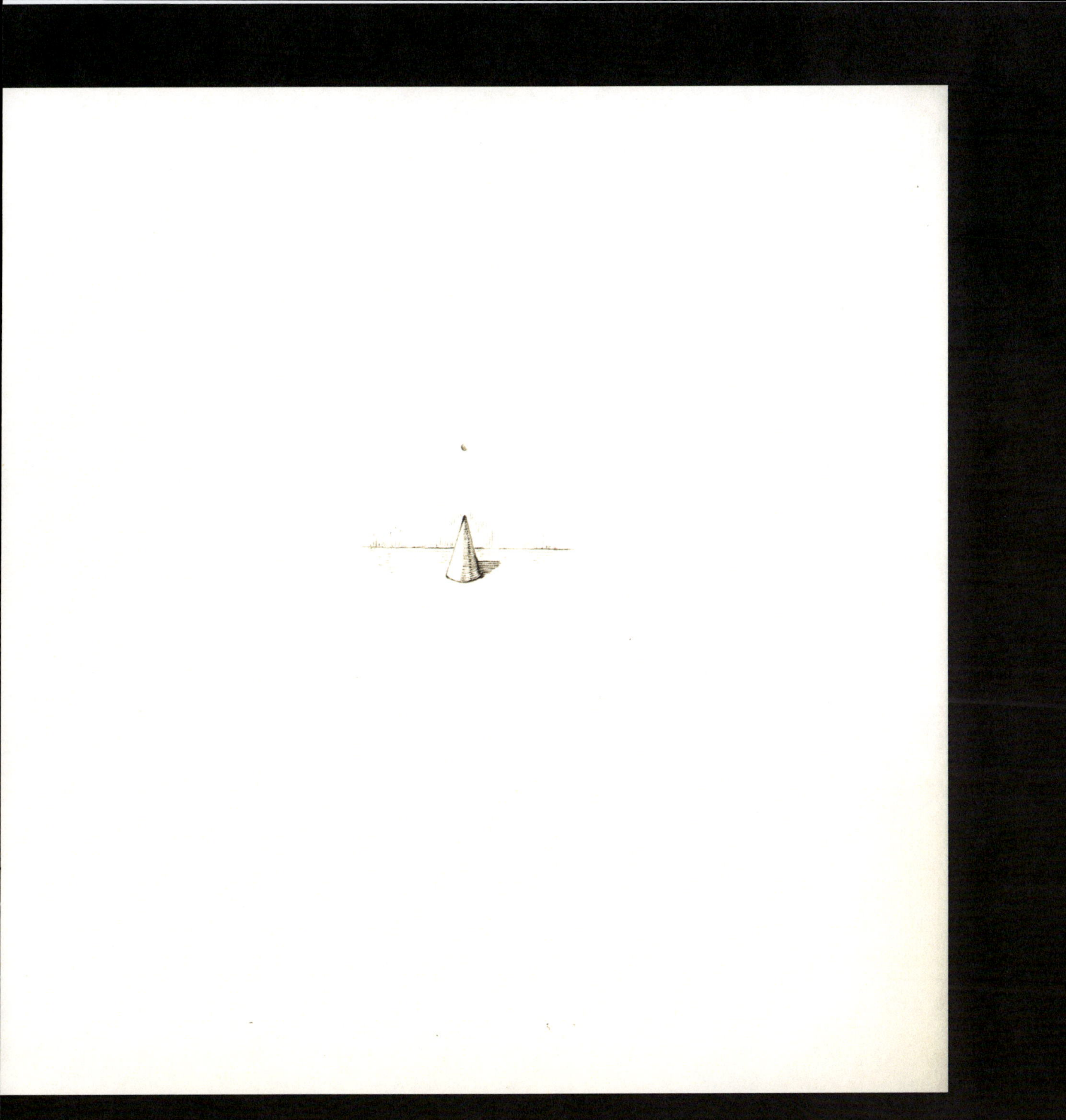

I learned the horizon's distance can be calculated
by your height above sea level.

The oldest, first to emerge, I was looking at a different distance than my sisters. Or the same view, differently.

I know, I know, so were they.

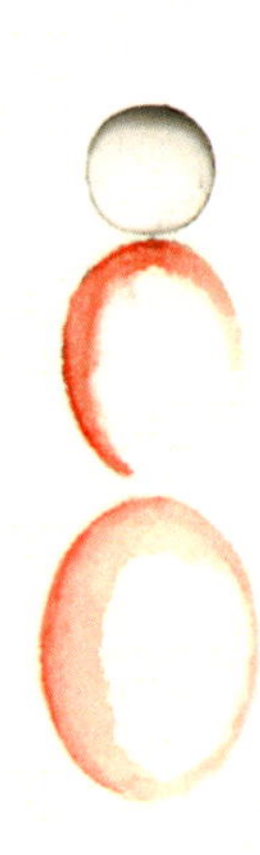

I did not know what, aside from me, was precarious.

But physics tells us that, once in motion, even the smallest things—
given length of run and type of terrain—can carve huge swaths.

We grew into other calculations. More complex math.

Our mother kept track of us on a tug-company calendar hung inside the
ironing board cupboard. Each boxed day was marked with the tide's sine
curve, predictable flood and ebb rising and falling across the weeks.

But (don't forget) all this was created by the moon.

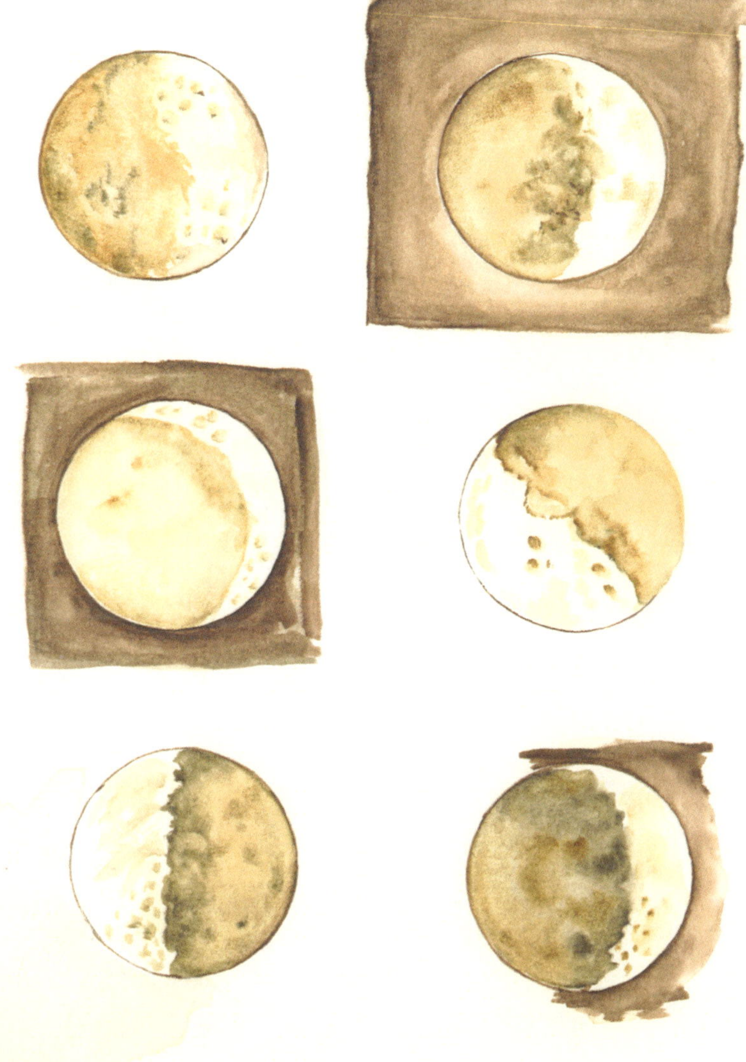

To cube is to find the ^{3} of x.

It is to leave the planar, the plain,

thus permitting shadow.

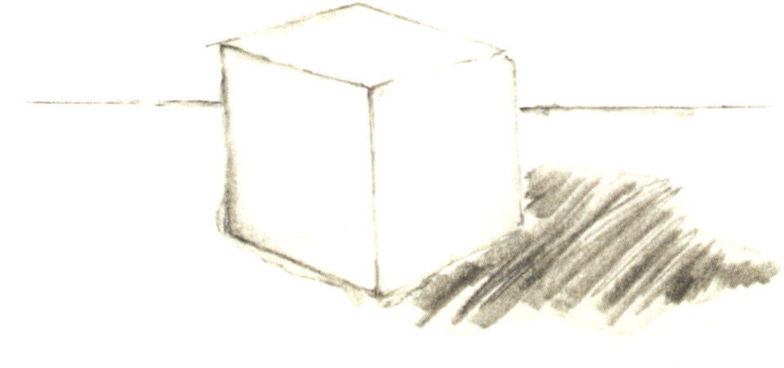

Our edges touched.   Our stories abutted.

The same light struck us at different times.

Something was on approach.

From elsewhere.

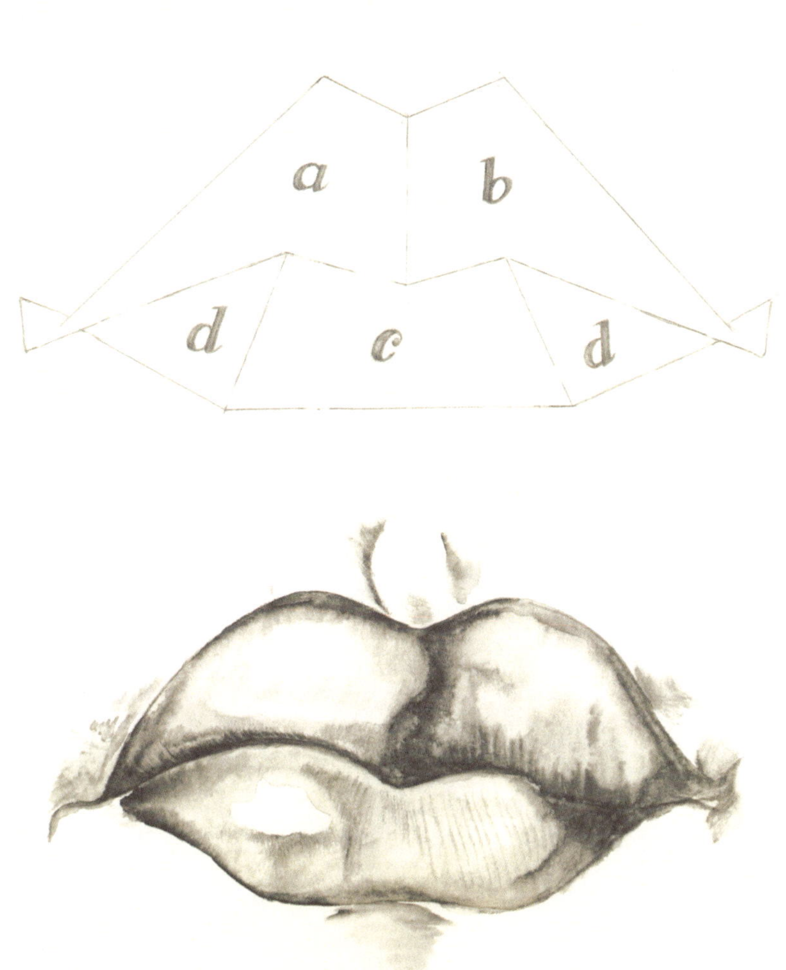

a
b
d
c
d

I was known as a secretive child.

Not at first, but later.

Maybe starting then.

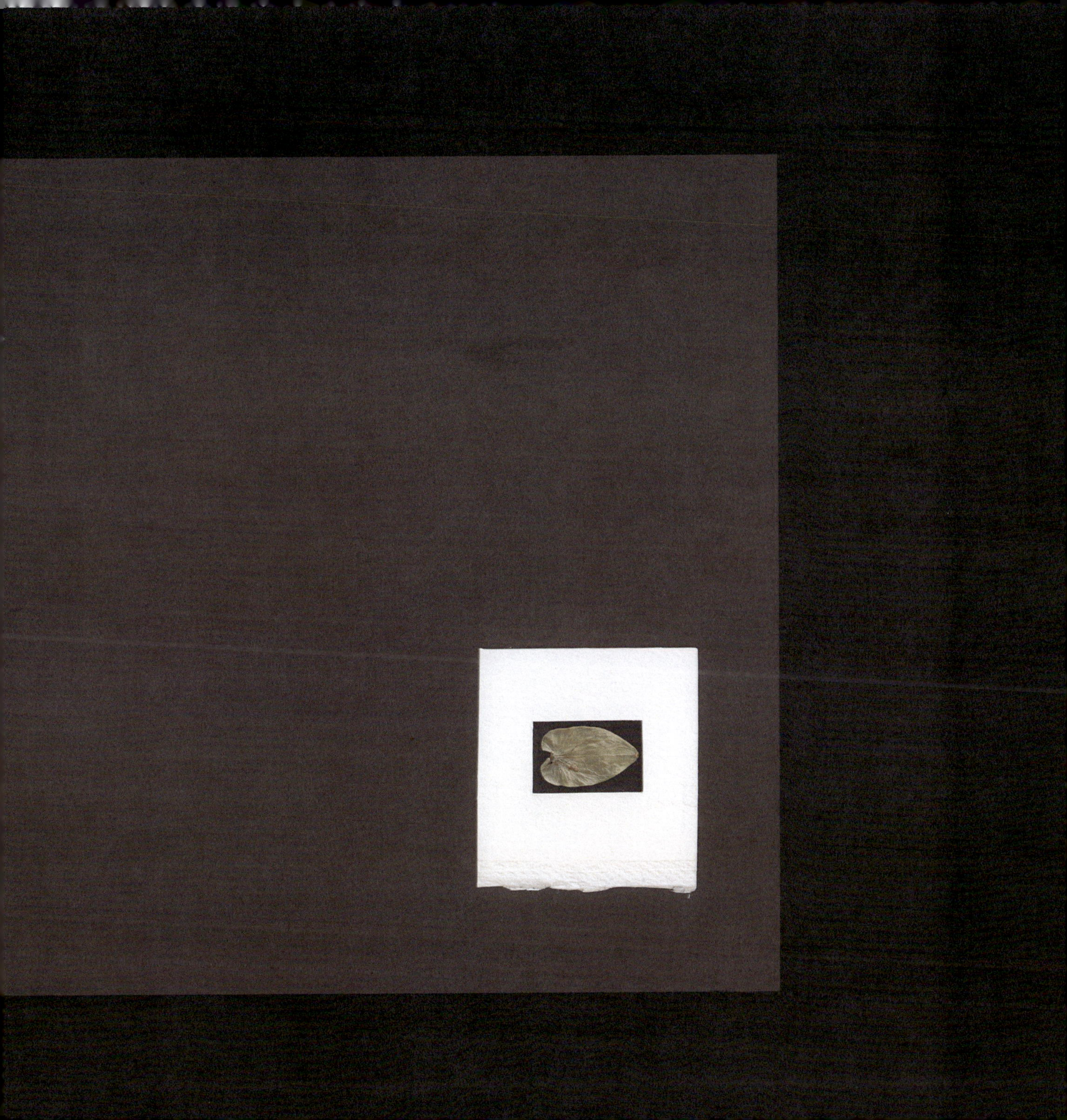

I could not find what was growing in me within any of the books on the shelves of our house. There was no guide available.

I could not identify, either, what was growing in my sisters alongside me. Or how, or why, or into what.

Photomorphs, we grew differently,

even as our roots all pulled from the same soil.

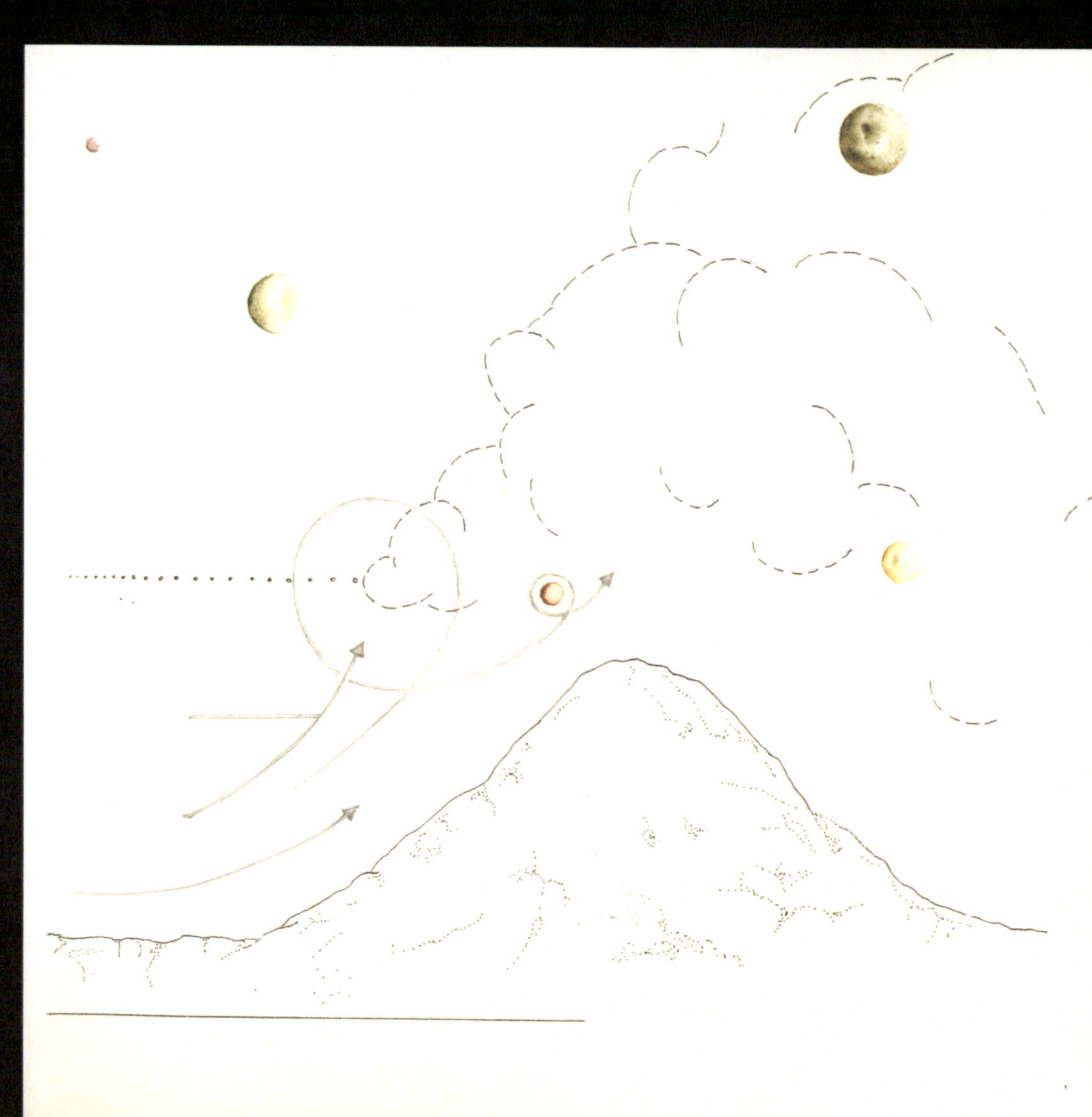

We lived on the wet side of western mountains yet
I don't really remember rain.

(I was very good at forgetting. I still am.)

I grappled with *rhumb lines*, arced routes that look longer
on the map but, my dad said, actually take less time to travel.

The math worked. But storms still howled out of who-
knows-where, shifting the courses of even huge ships.

How were my sisters navigating?
I didn't think to wonder.

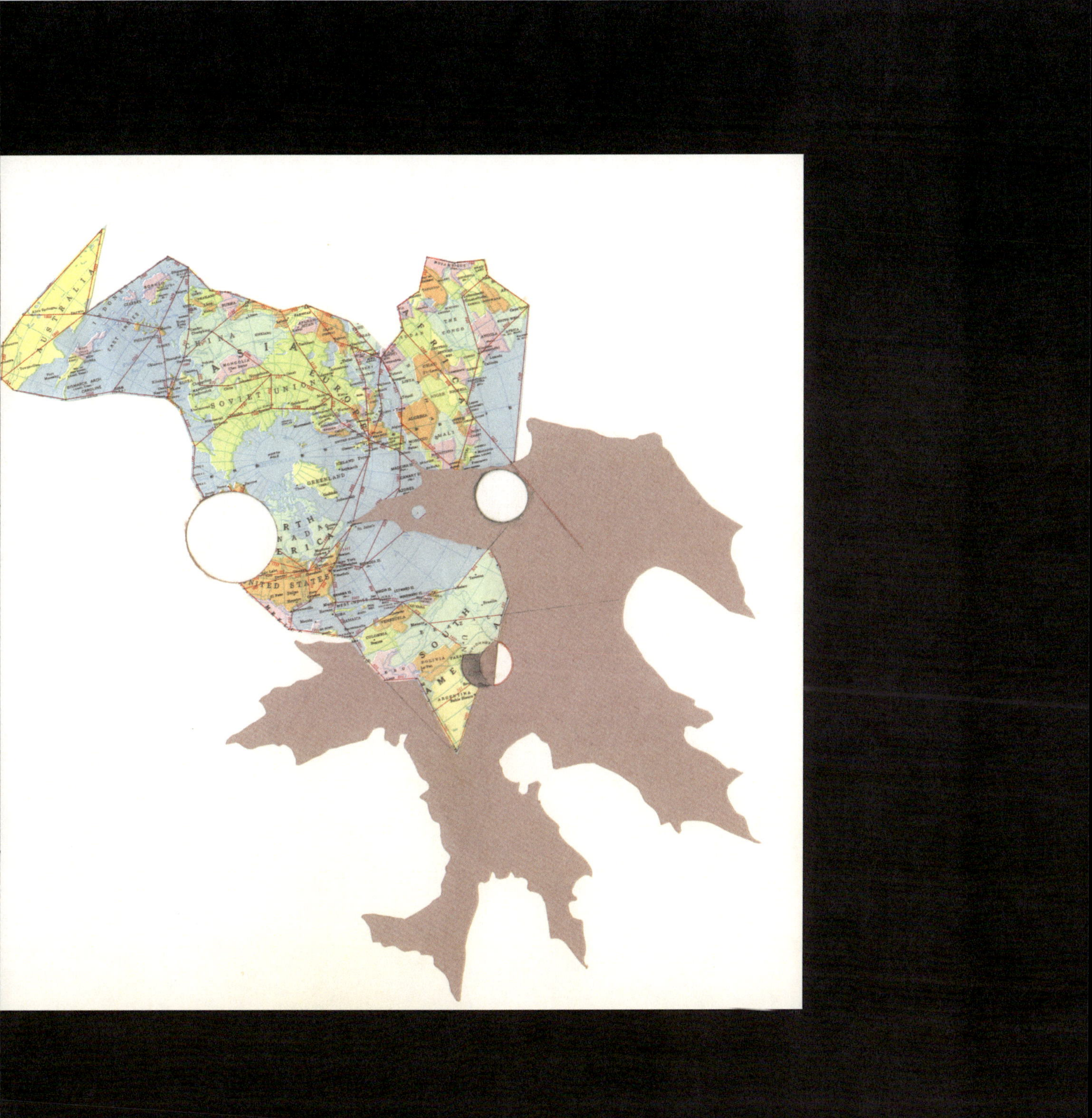

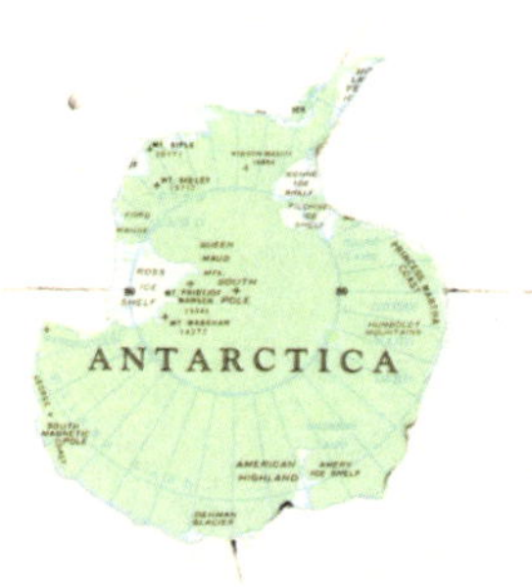
ANTARCTICA

No flat map shows the world's true shape.

We mis-learn extremities and peripheries from the start.

What else have I erased?

How can I know?

(This is the only way I can write about it.)

(The only way I will.)

(I promise.)

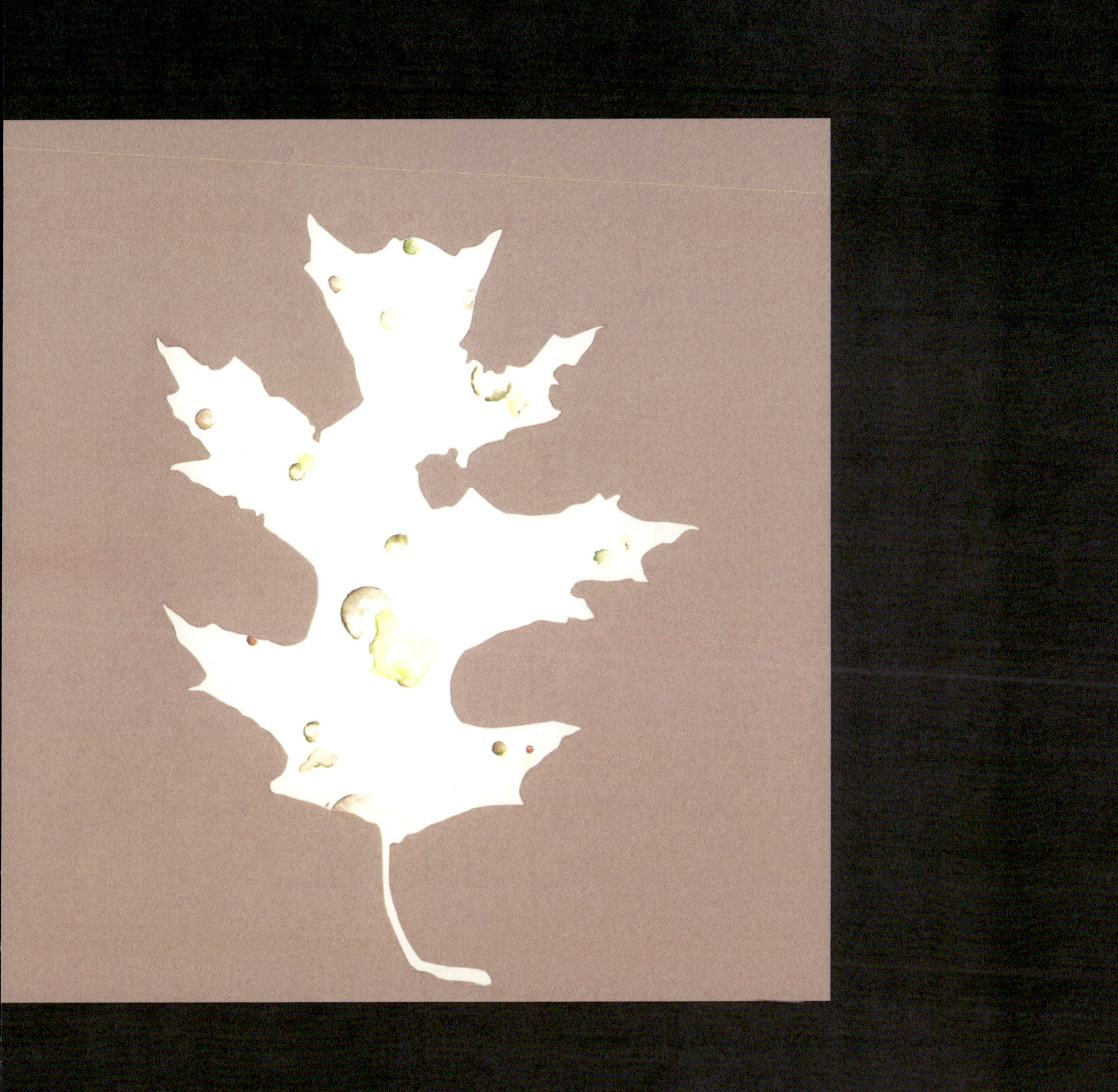

One secret has stepped into light,
has long glowed luminous.

How ridiculous now, its early, confused fear.

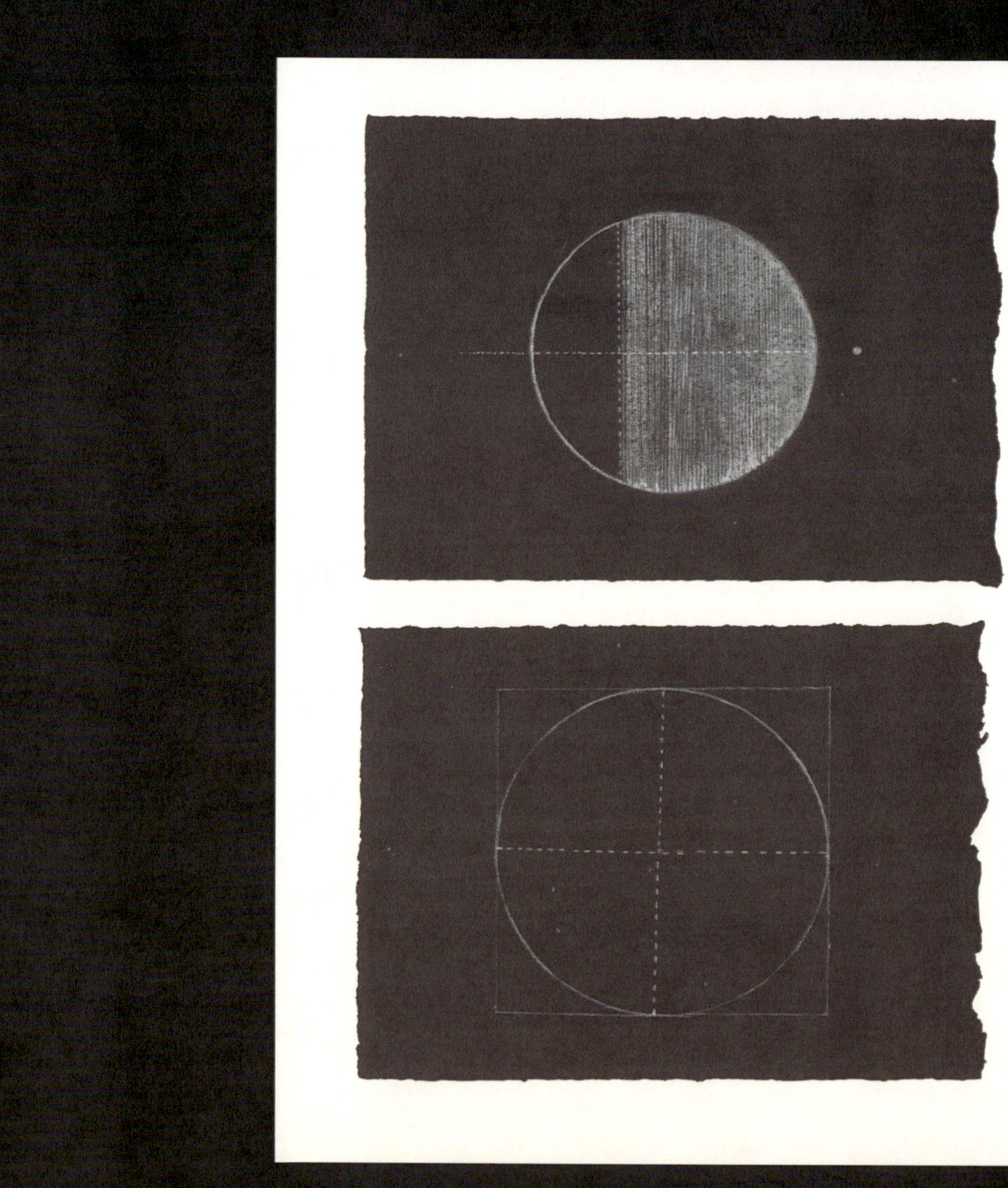

The other is not mine to tell.

                    A dark, dense absence

        a singularity

I can only measure what it has bent,
the adjustments made to avoid its pull.

It ghosts me.

Is there a truth it holds?

Too close for any perspective or clarity, how
can I ever know?

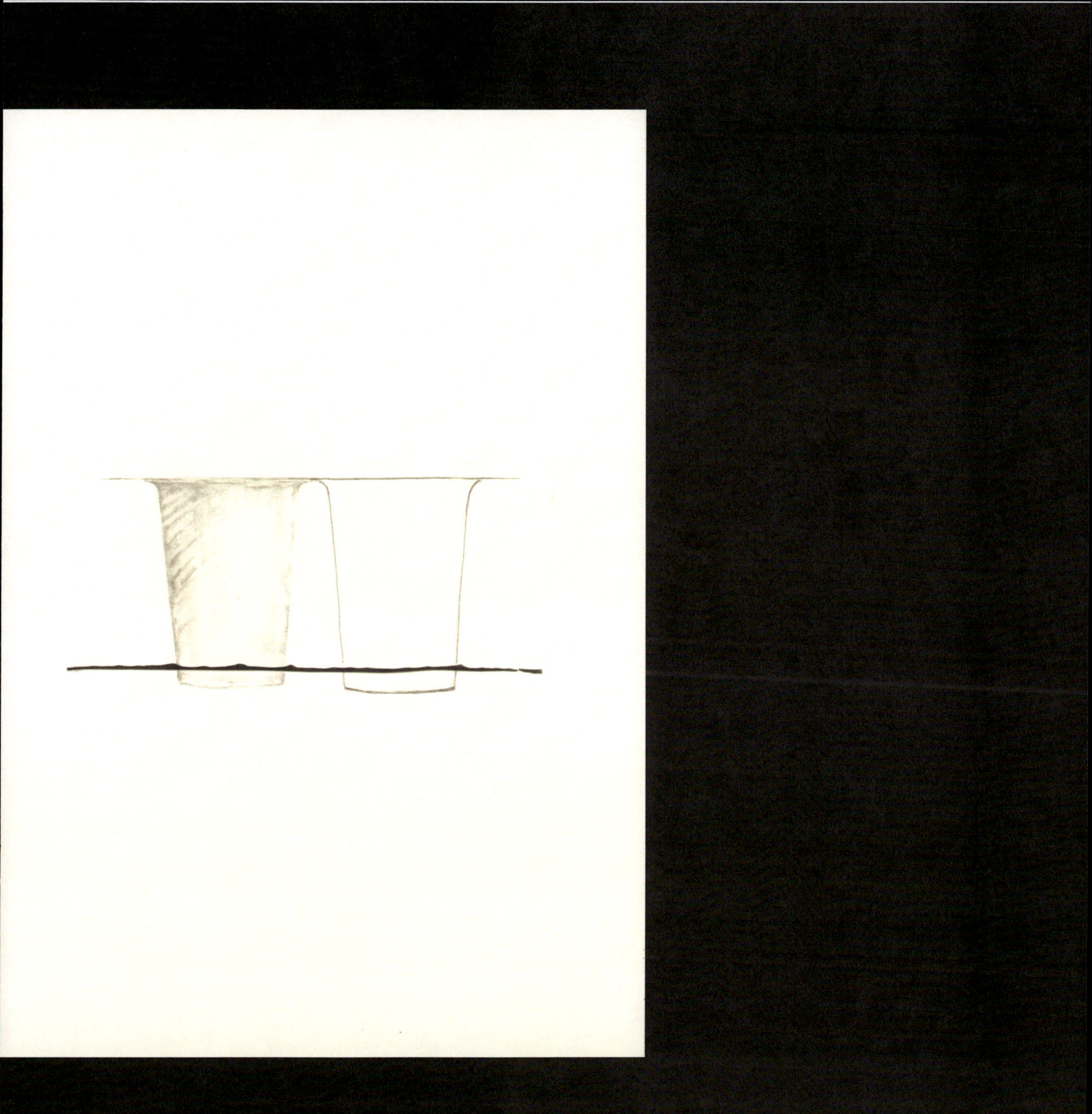

Look: I can pretend to see things two ways.
But the gut is singular and stubborn.

It knows what it first knew as true.

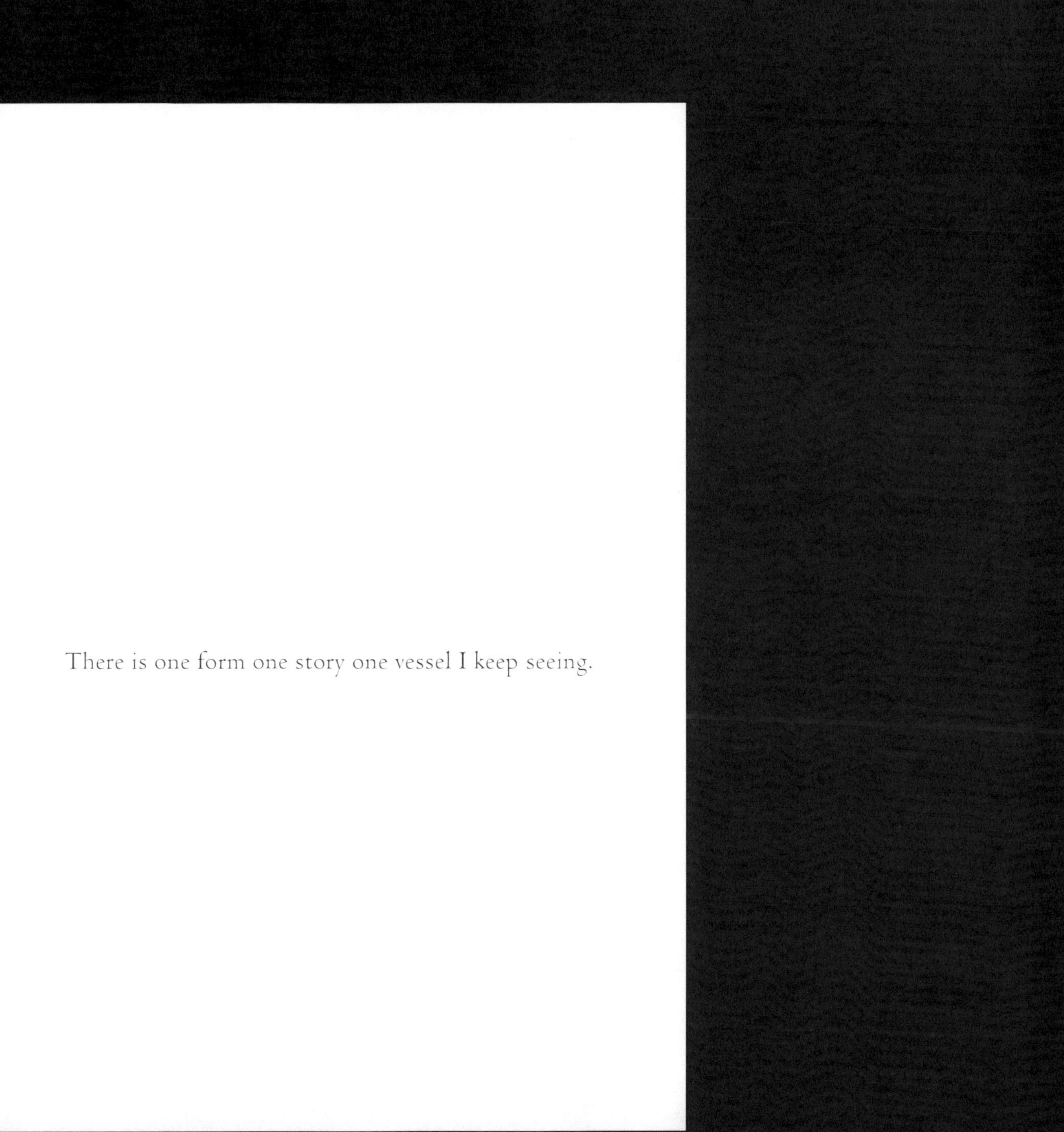

There is one form one story one vessel I keep seeing.

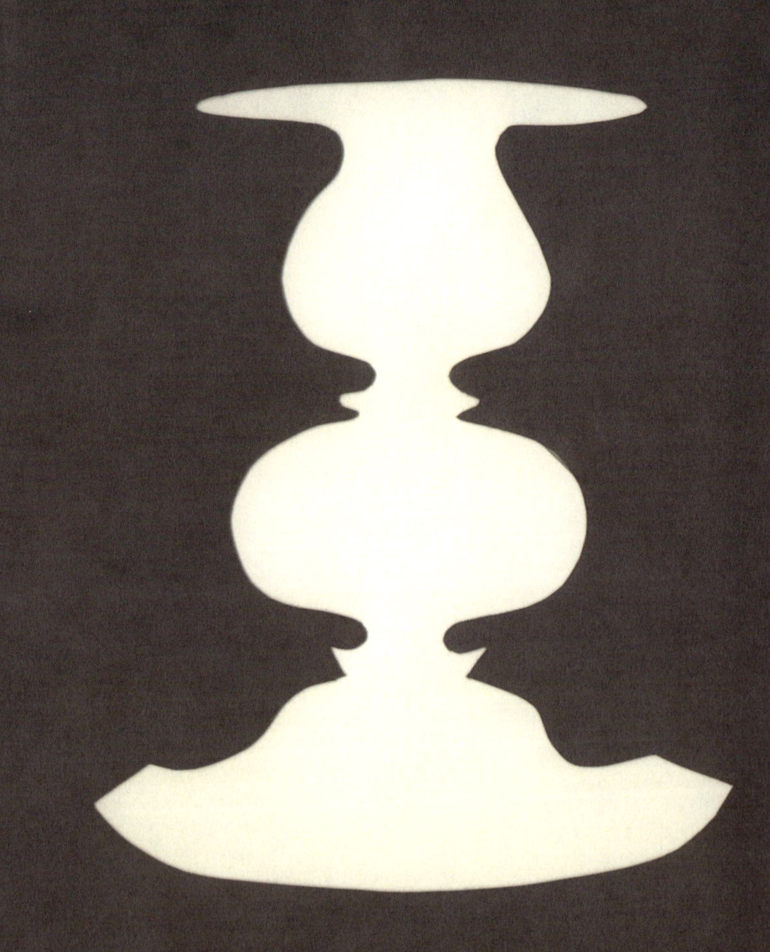

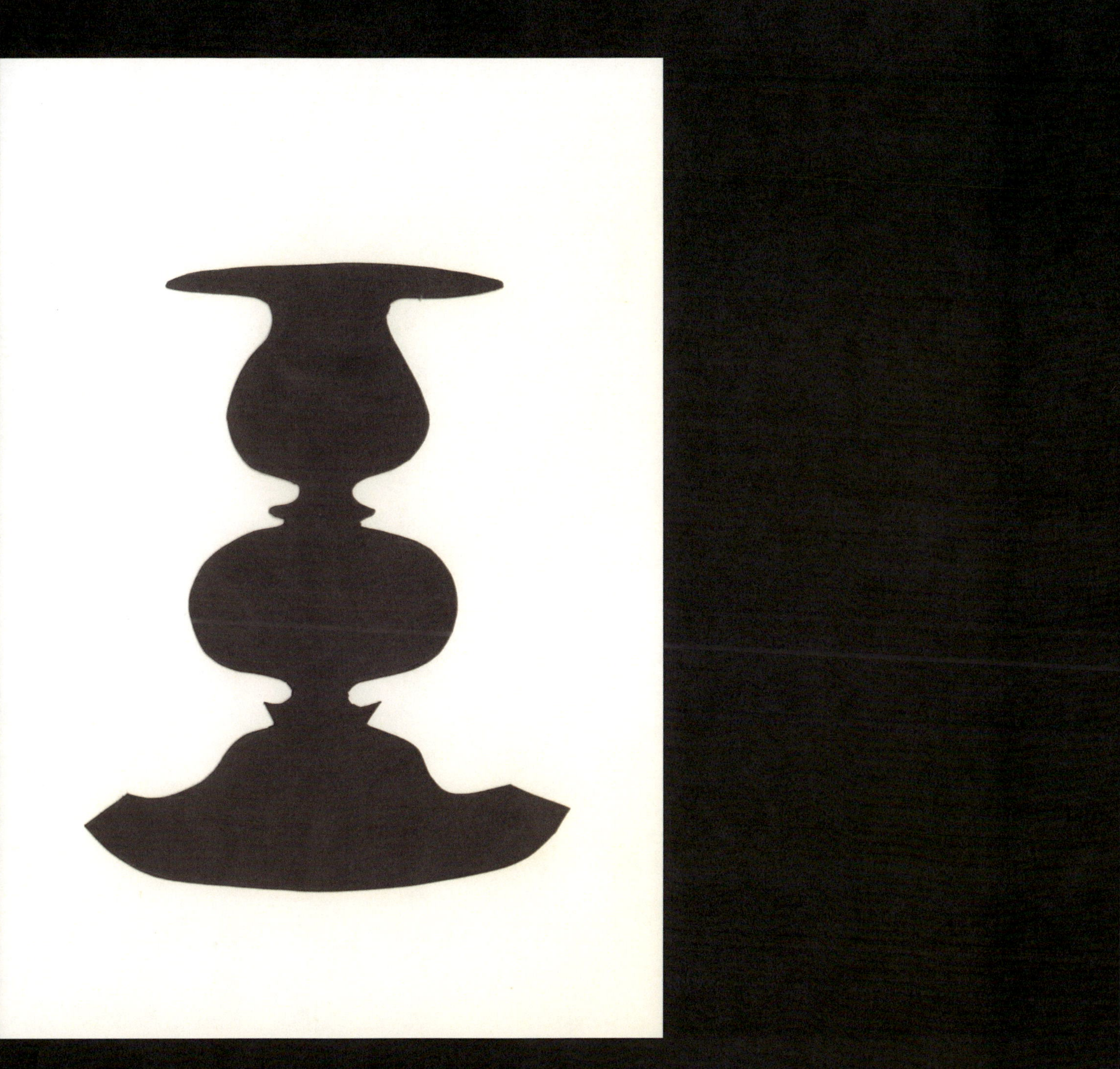

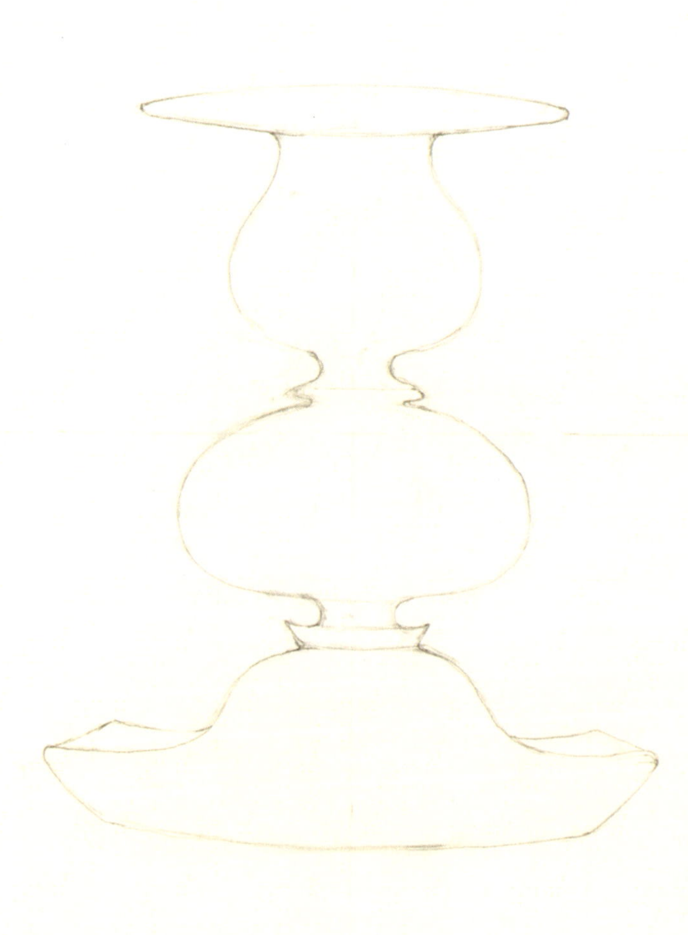

And, really, it is two stories
(2 cubed?) unfolding at once.

Recombinant.

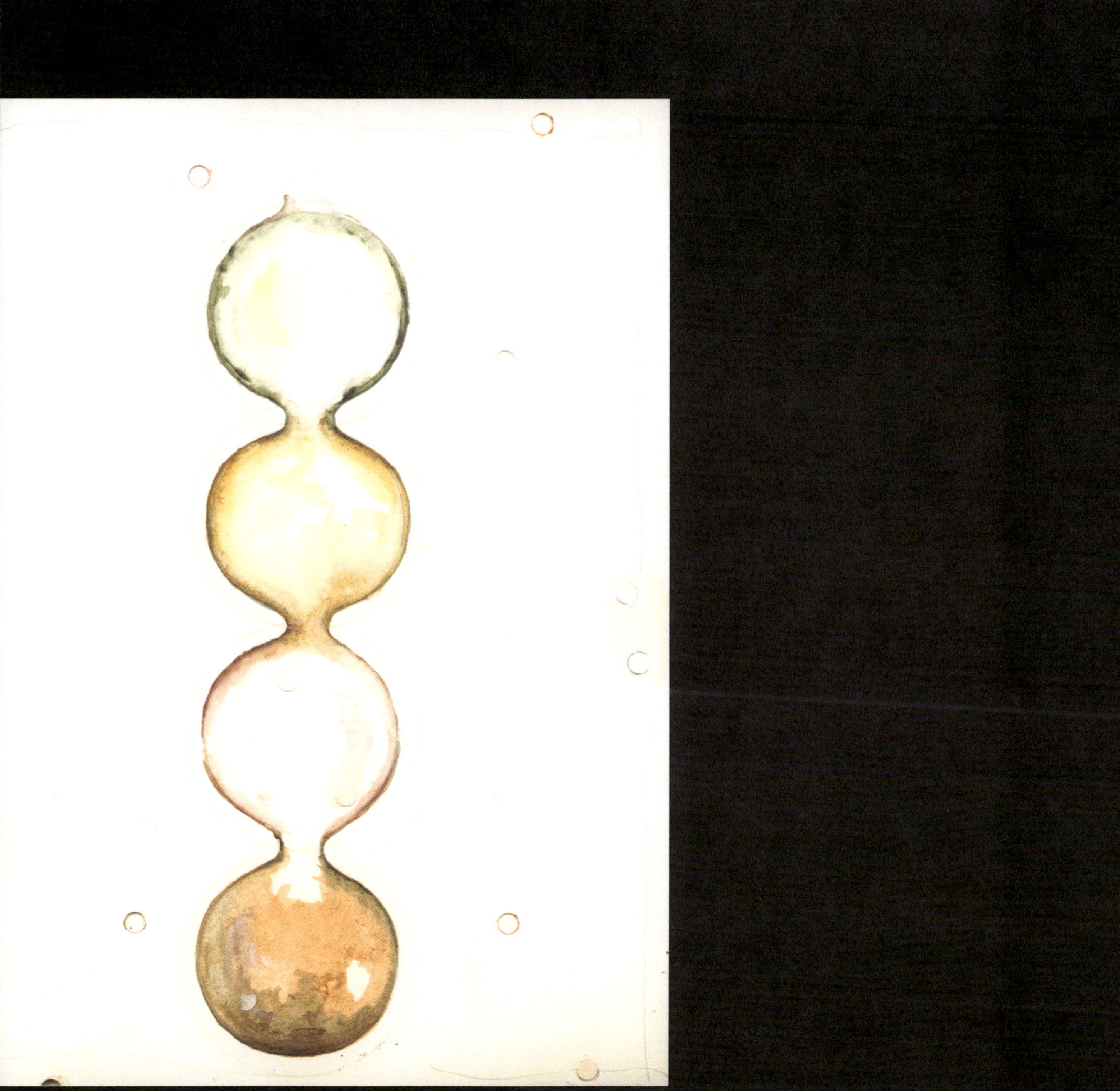

Flowing into and through each other.

Forging a unique amalgam.

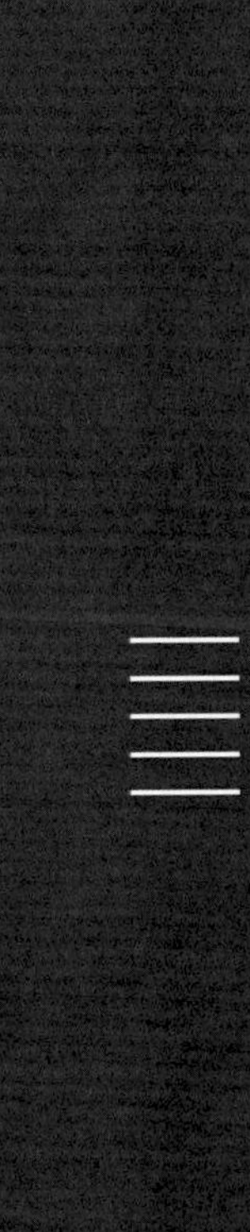

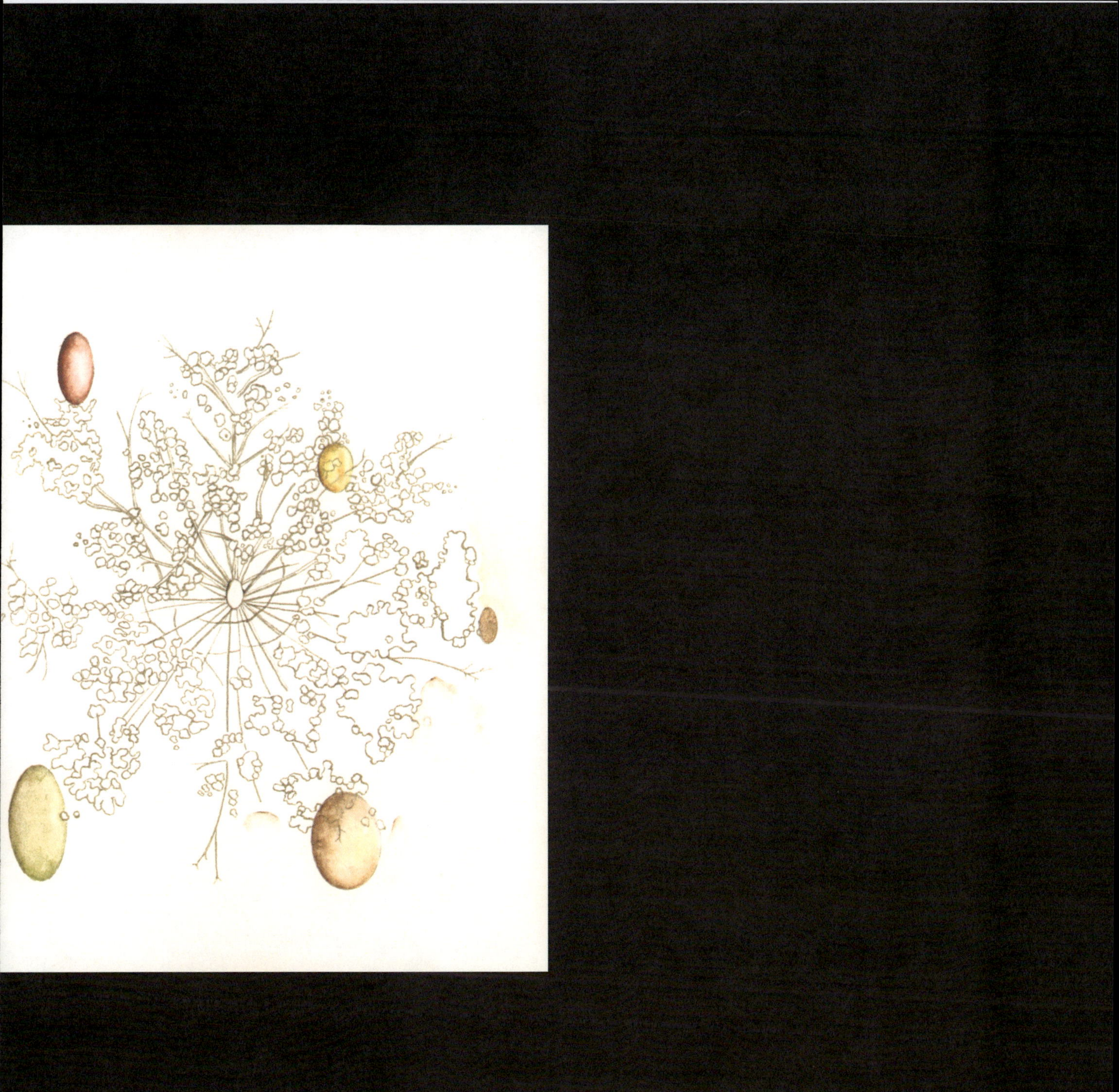

There were five of us. And a dog.
Only one dog at a time.

No one else.

The results are fractal.
The trajectories radiate.

Something happened.

To me and yet not to me.

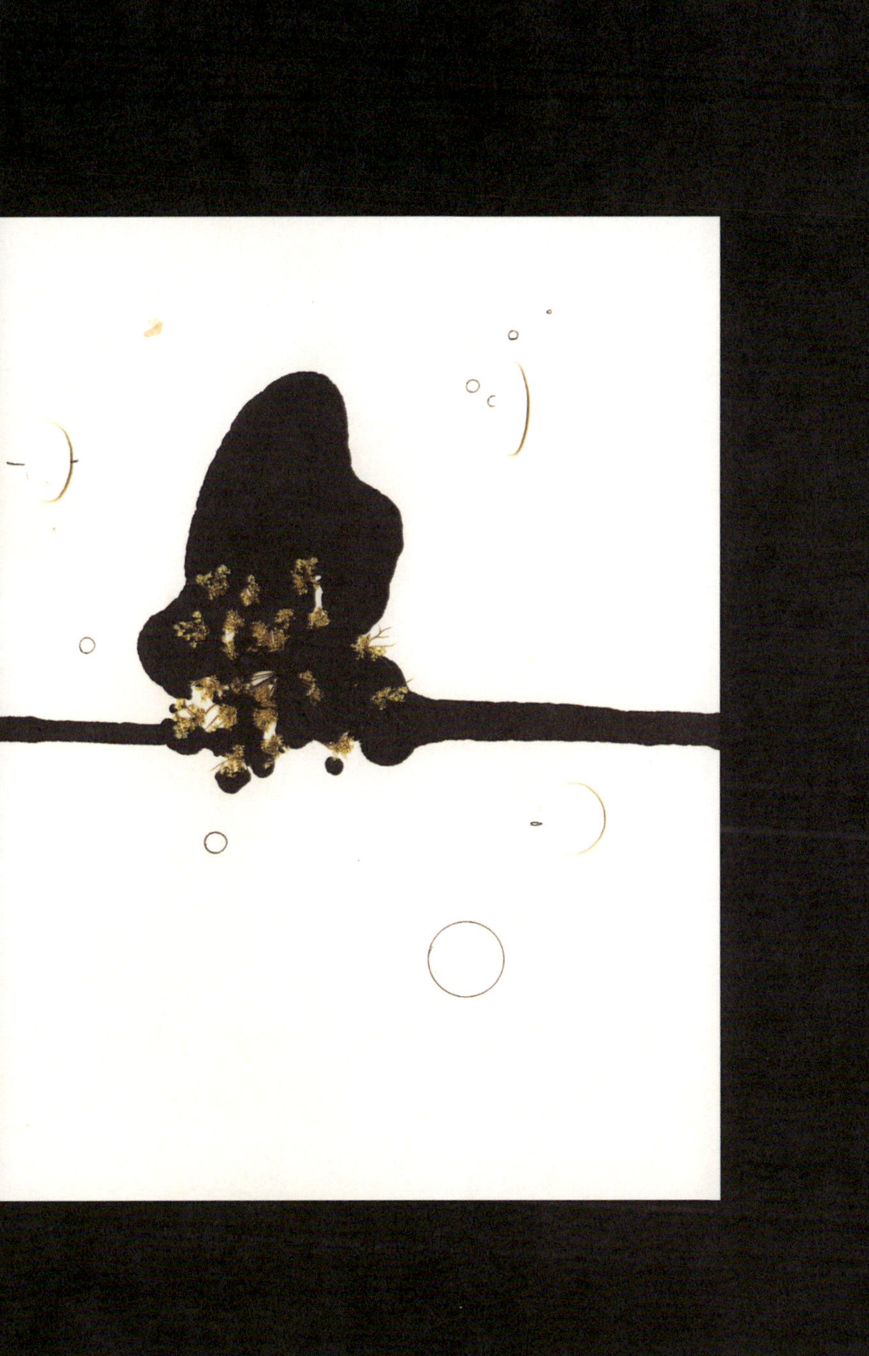

It divides absolutely.

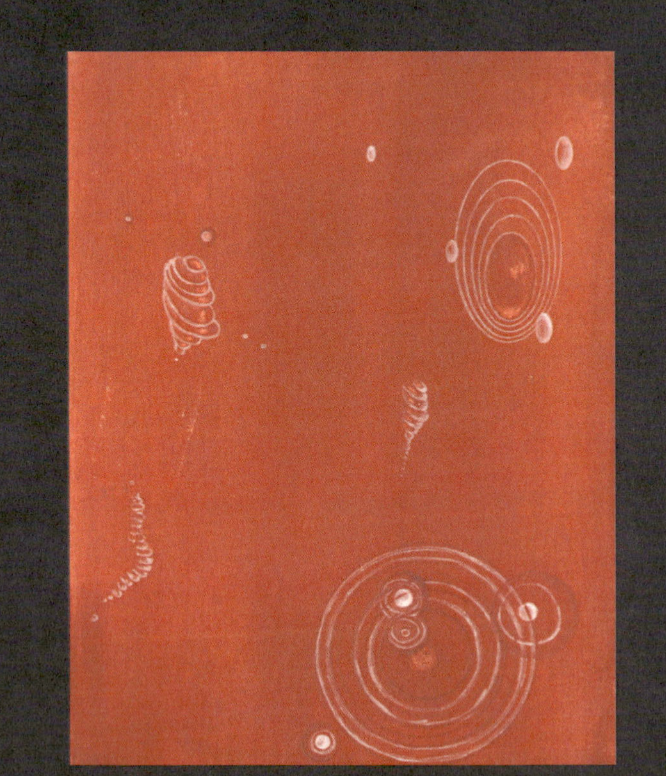

What was created in its chaos, light, dust, shadow

for me, for my sisters, for us all?

I am still trying to map it.

I am still trying to calculate what can be traced

to its redshifted source.

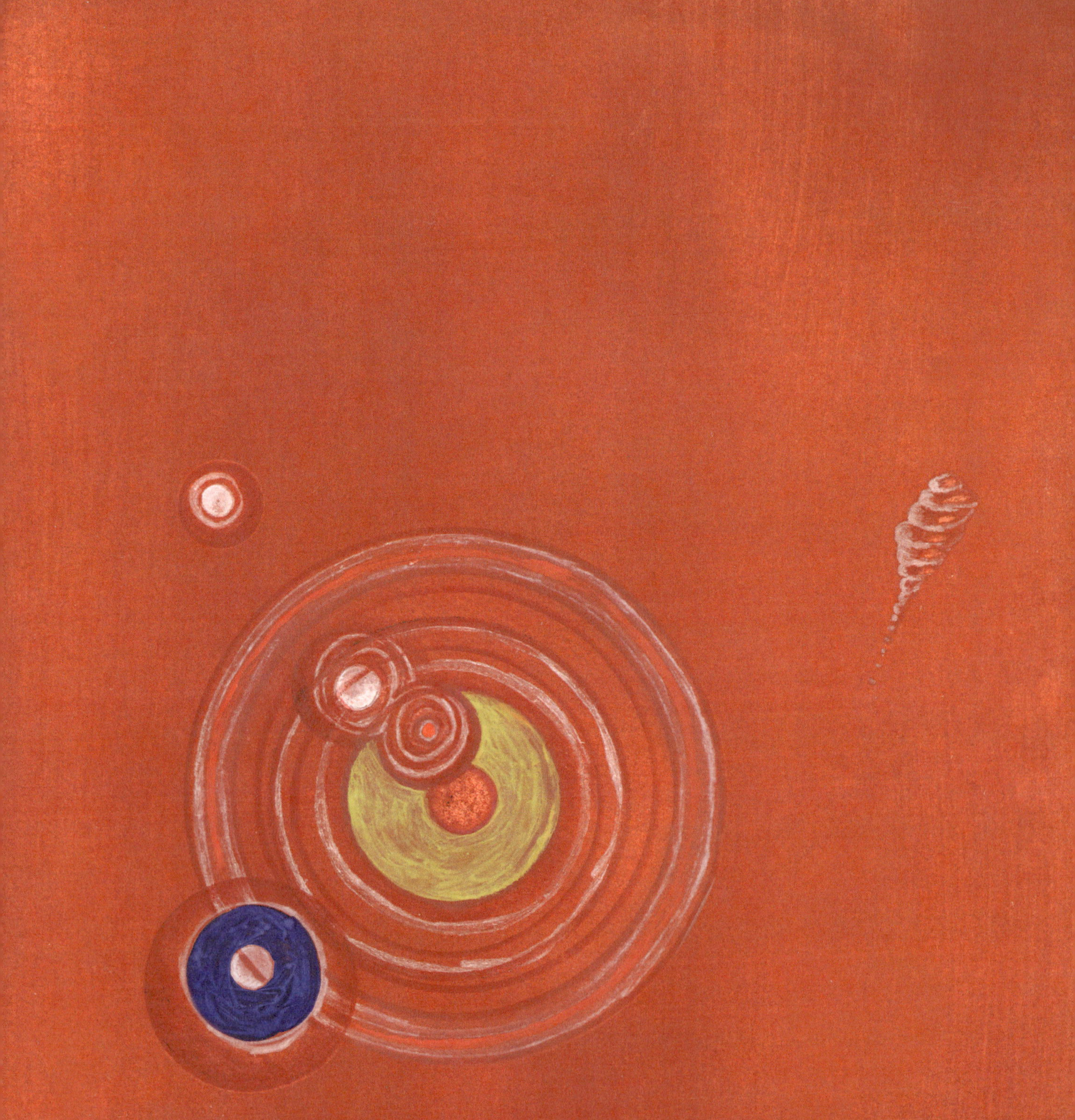

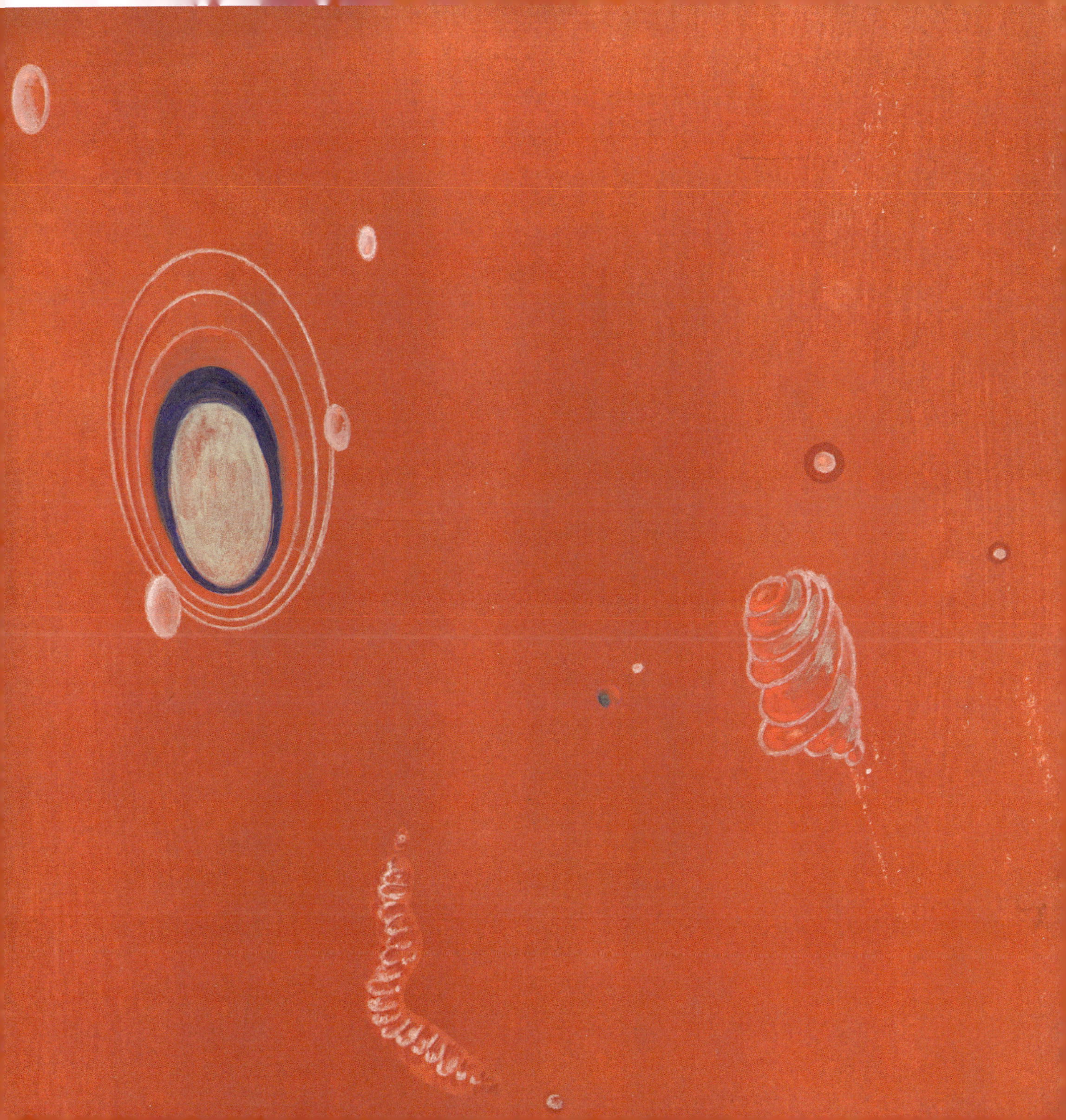

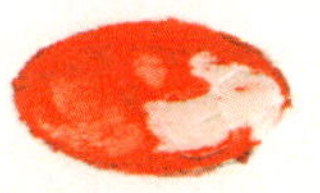

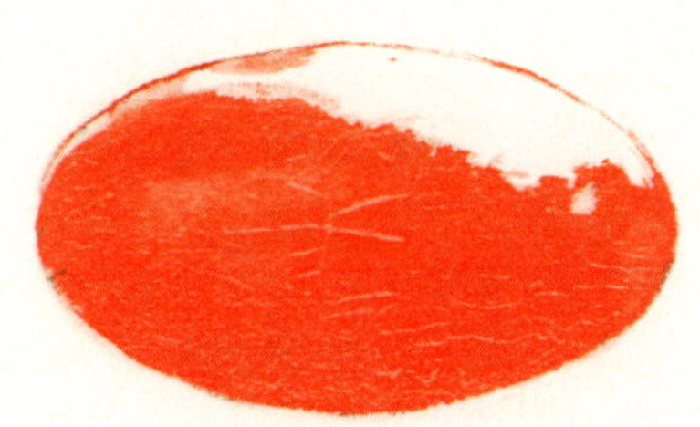

AFTERWORD

THEOREM

A general proposition not self-evident but proved by a chain of reasoning; a truth established by means of accepted truths. Via late Latin from Greek theōrēma 'speculation, proposition,' from theōrein 'look at,' from theōros 'spectator.'

Two types of telling can, in combination, open a universe.

AXIOM

A statement or proposition on which an abstractly defined structure is based. From Greek axiōma 'what is thought fitting,' from axios 'worthy.'

"Let's collaborate."

We began this exploration after years of seeking the right place to begin. Antonia suggested that *Ex Libris*, a book she had created, might open our conversation. We turned pages together. We talked. We listened to the paper under our fingers. We considered what was suggested by the images and form:

Revelations. Being revealed. Extraction. Excavation—the bottom of a hole; sand falling down on you as you dig. Toward dream? Winnowing. Telescoping. Different lenses for different scopes/scapes/selves. Revealed/ hidden/collapsing/expanding.

And then we parted. Elizabeth wrote a draft of what is here now and, over time and conversation, this theorem developed. This threnody. Word and image influencing, pushing, urging, questioning each other. Artist and writer finding new ways to articulate what is embedded in what they create.

PROOF

An inferential argument for a mathematical statement. In the argument, other previously established statements, such as theorems, can be used. In principle, a proof can be traced back to self-evident or assumed statements, known as axioms, along with accepted rules of inference.

Multiple significant things can happen simultaneously in a life, each profound on their own and in combination exponentially so. Their details need not be known to grasp their significance.

We want and need to leave things out of our stories in order to find clarity or peace. Winnowing is an act of survival. Yet the unsaid still thrums even as what's spoken narrows. Perhaps it even thrums more keenly. And such a thing is palpable beneath the scrim of what is offered as story, as self.

LAGRANGE'S THEOREM (MODIFIED)

Let AE be a finite group, and let E be a subgroup of A. Then the order of A divides the order of E.

How do you separate the subgroups? How do you mark the divisions? There is no perfect way. Events divide us. Events connect us. To others and to ourselves.

We create the maps of our lives from our remembered pasts, either following routes or avoiding them, plotting what course we can.

Elizabeth Bradfield & Antonia Contro

Cape Cod & Chicago

June, 2019

GRATITUDE

Many friends and supporters contributed to the evolution of *Theorem*. We are grateful for their encouragement, suggestions, and assistance. This collaboration could not have found its true expression without their help. We'd like, in particular, to acknowledge the following: Natalie Mills Bontumasi, Eliza Brown, Nickole Brown, Christine Byl, Chris Cotten, Laura Donnelley, Mary Ittelson, Jessica Jacobs, Clara Lyon, George Marquisos, Joseph E. Merideth, Debbie Nadolney, Janice Redman, Alexandra Teague, Sarah Van Sanden, Lisa Sette, Philip Yenawine, Lori Zimmerman, and all the Bradfields.

Support from Good Works Foundation and the Theodore and Jane Norman Fund from Brandeis University fueled the early stages of this work, as did a generous gift from Helen Zell. A fine art, letterpressed, hand-bound limited edition of *Theorem* was published by Candor Arts in the fall of 2019. Working with their dedicated, creative, and talented team was a privilege. Finally, we are most grateful for the time, care, and support of Poetry Northwest Editions—particularly Kevin Craft and Abi Pollokoff, who have made a beautiful home and editorial family for *Theorem*.

ELIZABETH BRADFIELD is the author of the poetry collections *Once Removed*, *Approaching Ice*, *Interpretive Work* and the mixed-genre *Toward Antarctica*, which pairs her photographs with brief, hybrid essays. Her poems and essays have appeared in *The New Yorker*, *West Branch*, *Orion* and many anthologies. She has been awarded a Stegner Fellowship, the Audre Lorde Prize, and was a finalist for the James Laughlin Award from the Academy of American Poets. Founder and editor-in-chief of Broadsided Press, she works as a naturalist and teaches creative writing at Brandeis University. www.ebradfield.com

ANTONIA CONTRO is a visual artist whose work ranges from discrete objects to site-specific installations and collaborations that engage artists and practitioners from a wide range of disciplines. Her art explores the nature of knowledge, memory, and time. Contro's exhibitions include *Tempus Fugit* at the American Philosophical Society Museum, *Ex Libris* at the Chicago Cultural Center, *Closed|Open* at the Newberry Library, and *Descry* at the Museum of Contemporary Photography. Contro's work is in the collections of the Art Institute of Chicago, the Block Museum, the Fogg Art Museum, the Museum of Contemporary Art, and others. Contro was awarded a Rockefeller Foundation fellowship, an Illinois Arts Council fellowship, and a doctorate in humanities *honoris causa* from Lewis University. www.antoniacontro.com

Poem text set in Venetian 301 BT
Book design by Natalie Mills Bontumasi
Printed on archival quality paper

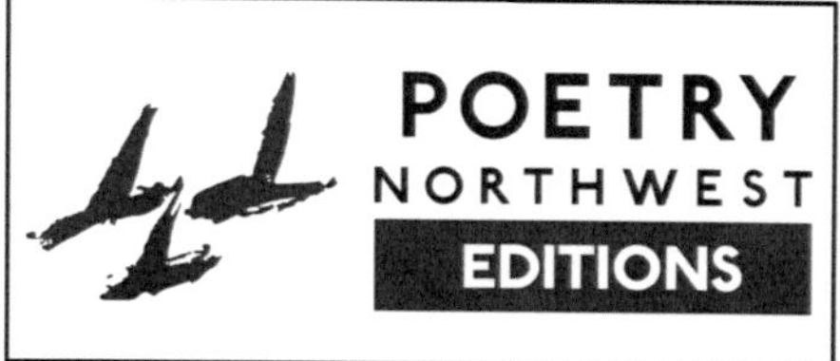

Poetry NW Editions is an independent, non-profit educational press in residence at Everett Community College. This book was edited and produced by Kevin Craft and Abi Pollokoff.